Caselets in Strategic Management

Author

Dr. Pratik C Patel

Copyright © 2020 by Dr. Pratik C Patel

All rights reserved. This book or any portion thereof may not be reproduced or used in any manner whatsoever without the express written permission of the author except for the use of brief quotations in a book review and research work.

© **Author**

About the Book

In today's economy, gaining and sustaining a competitive advantage is harder than ever. But there are few companies which have been able to make a mark in this cut through competition also through their innovative and creative strategies. This book is a collection of Caselets of such companies from across the globe.

The Caselets discussed in this book will be of immense help to the budding managers in developing various skills like decision making and problem solving and creativity.

Dr. Pratik C Patel

The book is dedicated to

Maa Saraswati

&

My beloved family

Contents

1.	Taking sneakers to the Air: The rise of Nike's Air Jordan brand	08
2.	Rise of IPhone and Demise of Nokia	12
3.	Creating your own ocean to swim alone through Blue Ocean Strategy	15
4.	Badge engineering	19
5.	Uber: Redefining the car rental industry	23
6.	Amazon Dash Button: Order Process Innovation	26
7.	Netflix redefining movie viewing experience through disruptive innovation	28
8.	Facebook's acquisition of Instagram; Strategy to Cornering a fledgling market	31
9.	The Toyota Way: the story of beating the big three of USA in their own backyard	34
10.	'Chai Calling': Engineering-background 'chai-wallas' are making crores via their desi start-up	36
11.	Dabbawalas of Mumbai: The Original Food Delivery Network in India	39
12.	FedEx: The overnight delivery service was anything but an overnight success	42
13.	Rolex Oyster: A crown worth for every achievement	46
14.	Lenskart: the journey towards becoming the largest online eye wear store in India	49
15.	Revitalizing the brand Harley Davidson through brand community	52

16.	How Ratan Tata brought life to fading Jaguar Land Rover	55
17.	How Canon beat xerox by using the New Lanchester Strategy	58
18.	The end of kodak moment: The story of how a legacy brand failed to keep pace with technology	61
19.	Meesho: The Indian social commerce site which attracted Facebook	64
20.	The new coke: How it became the biggest strategic blunder in consumer goods industry	66
21.	The turnaround of Royal Enfield brand	69
22.	Airbnb: the journey towards becoming the biggest startup of 21st century	72
23.	Saying Tata to Zica: The case of branding going wrong	76
24.	Pepsi Blue: one of the biggest failures for PepsiCo	79
25.	Pepsi Next: A soft drink for the next generation	81
26.	Paytm pioneering the E Wallet business in India through innovative strategies	84
27.	Amazon redefining online retailing with Amazon Prime membership	87
28.	Paradigm shift in Hotel Industry due to technology	91
29.	Cadbury Celebrations - Eating into the traditional sweets' market through innovative marketing strategies	94
30.	Kizashi: A rare failure for Maruti Suzuki in India	98
31.	The end of the road for Indian icon "Ambassador"	102
32.	Fall of Bajaj Chetak: A case of Marketing Myopia	106

33.	Coca Cola acquisition of Thumps Up: A lesson in globalization	109
34.	TravelSpice	113

1.

TAKING SNEAKERS TO THE AIR: THE RISE OF NIKE'S AIR JORDAN BRAND

Shoes were just shoes for the first 80 odd years of the 20th century until the mid-1980s when Nike redefined the rule of the game by releasing a pair of shoes featuring Michael Jordan named "Air Jordan".

"Air Jordans", now commonly known as Jordan Brand has a long and rich history starting from 1985 when the first model was released, **the Air Jordan 1**. It was created for then NBA player and 5 times NBA MVP (Most Valuable Player) Michael Jordan. At that time Michael Jordan was just the new comer but Nike saw the potential in this player and invested in him. After being selected as third overall pick by the Chicago Bulls in 1984, Michael Jordan was signed by Nike to a five-year deal worth $2.5 million, a hefty price tag at that time. Nike gave Jordan his own signature and the Nike Air Jordan was born. Over a period of time the Air Jordan became the most sought-after sneaker in the country and an immortal icon of the times.

The first Air Jordan pair was sold for $65, which were by far the most expensive basketball shoes in the market at that time. These shoes now regularly sell for $200 or more per pair while certain models even fetch thousands of dollars when they're released in low supplies. In 2016, the Jordan brand alone brought in close to $3 billion in revenue for Nike. That's roughly 35% of the total revenue of the entire company.

But the journey wasn't at all fun and simple. In 1985 NBA Commissioner David Stern fined Michael Jordan for wearing the **"Air Jordan 1"** in black and red due to not meeting the NBA's dress code (The white only shoes). Then onwards each time Michael wore them, he would be fined $5,000.

A usual action from any corporate in such situation would have been to recall the colorful shoes to comply with the authority but Nike thought otherwise. Nike saw this action of fining Michael Jordan as a blessing in disguise and took on a perfect marketing ploy. They decided to pay Jordan's fines and released a commercial giving this pair the nickname "Banned". This "Banned" advertisement created the much-needed buzz around the brand "Air Jordan" and made it one of the most sought-after sneaker brands. The buzz was so strong that in the first year of launch itself; more than 3 million pairs of Air Jordan were sold against the actual projection of 100,000 pairs by Nike itself.

Then onwards each year, a new Air Jordan is unveiled. Each unveiling has met with ever increasing anticipation from the media, industry, and the buying public. Air Jordans ever since its inception dominate the market in sales and demand, with each year's model establishing higher benchmark for standards in design, innovation and performance for the entire athletic footwear industry.

Michael Jordan wore "Air Jordan" throughout his illustrious career that epitomizes his relentless dedication to performance, innovation and achievement. Over a period of time **Michael Jordan** became the greatest player in the history of basketball and the **"Air Jordan"** became the most successful sneaker brand in the history. Michael Jordan has since made $1.3 billion just from royalty for Air Jordan.

Nike's Jordan Brand used celebrity collaborations to overcome a dip in the rankings and keep its reputation as the most iconic sneaker brand of all time.

Michael Jordan wearing Air Jordan

"Banned" as they promoted initially.

Caselets in Strategic Management

2.

RISE OF IPHONE AND DEMISE OF NOKIA

Many new products are able to break through in the established market by bringing innovation and thinking out of the box (e.g. iPhone) and many existing brands are thrown out due to their inability to keep pace with changing market trend, Nokia is one such example.

Nokia is one of the companies who pioneered mobile phone industry and ruled the global cell phone market for years. It was the first company that transformed cell phones into fashion accessories and brought mobile to everyone's reach. Despite the fact that at its peak in 2008 it had staggering 40% global market share; the brand Nokia began to decline and finally collapsed in the year 2013.

But what made the once leading brand to die? Nokia died because of its complacency; Nokia remained indifferent when others were rewriting the rule of the game and paid the price.

World Mobile market show a major change in the year 2007 when Apple introduced iPhone. Apple realised that Nokia and BlackBerry were already making fantastic phones and probably they were unbeatable so it decided not to make cell phones. Apple decided to change the rules of the game so it didn't create a phone that was also smart, something that BlackBerry and Nokia were doing. Rather it created a smart device that was also a phone. The Apple iPhone was a small pocketable computer. Primarily it was meant to calculate and process data, the way computers do. It could run apps, or in other words computer programs. The fact that it could also connect to cellular network and make calls was just the icing on the cake.

A year later, Android from Google not only followed in the footsteps of iPhone but also expanded on the idea of pocketable computers and launched Android Phones. Google's Android was even more flexible like modern computers, and allowed a user to do more, the way computers do. Since then, both Apple and Google have constantly worked to make iPhones and Android devices more and more powerful. They worked to enable more powerful hardware in their devices.

Nowadays, a good Android phone or an iPhone can handle many tasks that earlier required a laptop. You can browse web, edit office documents, edit images or videos, play 3D games and watch Full HD videos and a lot more on these devices.

Nokia and BlackBerry failed to grasp this. Even years after iPhone was introduced, they were still trying to compete in the market with phones that have smart features whereas people preferred to buy small computers that can also make calls.

Apple was able to pull off this revolution because it was a rare breed: a computer company equally devoted to both hardware and software. Nokia on the other side was a hardware company that never fully grasped the software business. Had Nokia realized its limitations, perhaps the brand "Nokia" would also have survived like the Samsung. The world's leader in Smartphone sales, Samsung, did relatively little innovations still it managed to survive by adapting the changes with time. Samsung borrowed liberally from Apple's innovations and used Google's Android platform for their smart phones. Samsung not only survived but beat Apple largely on price and became leader in world Smartphone market. Lately Nokia also tried to change by moving its devices to Windows but it was too late.

Nokia died because "It was a very good phone company but a very poor computer company".

3.

CREATING YOUR OWN OCEAN TO SWIM ALONE THROUGH BLUE OCEAN STRATEGY

Every company wants to have but a very few companies have one; A compelling Strategy.

W. Chan Kim & Renee Mauborgne

In the era of globalization and cut through competition, it is very difficult for a new firm to enter in an industry and develop leadership. It is even more difficult when market is already dominated by existing players. But few firms manage to break the ice and sail through with their unique strategy. One such strategy is "Blue Ocean Strategy".

Blue Ocean Strategy was first coined by W. Chan Kim & Renee Mauborgne in their book titled "Blue Ocean Strategy". They coined two terms 'Red oceans' and 'Blue oceans' to denote the market universe in their book.

Red oceans are all the industries in existence today; the known market space where industry boundaries are defined and companies try to outperform their rivals to grab a greater share of the existing market. Cutthroat competition turns the ocean bloody red. Hence, its termed as 'red' oceans.

Blue oceans denote all the industries not in existence today; the unknown market space, unexplored and untainted by competition. Like the 'blue' ocean, it is vast, deep and powerful in terms of opportunity and profitable growth.

The aim of **Blue ocean strategy** is to open up a new market space and create new demand. It is about creating and capturing uncontested market space and thereby making the competition irrelevant by introducing an innovative product or product with superior features. It is based on the view that market boundaries and industry structure are not given and can be constructed by the actions and beliefs of industry players.

To create blue ocean is obviously a difficult task but it is highly rewarding as it helps the company to make huge profits; as the company can charge little higher because of its unique and superior features. There are few companies who could do it and got benefitted.

Apple iTunes is one such example. Apple entered into the digital music industry in 2003 with its product iTunes. With the introduction of this product, it becomes easy for the Apple users to download original and high-quality music at a reasonable price. iTunes created an easy and convenient way of distributing music by making traditional sources of distribution of music irrelevant. Earlier CDs (compact disks) were used to distribute and listen to music. With iTunes, Apple succeeded in capturing the rising demand of users for the quality music. All the products of Apple that were available in the market have iTunes for users to download music.

Canon is another company which smartly used blue ocean strategy and created personal desktop copier industry. Traditionally copier machines were meant for office purchasers only; who required machines that are durable, fast, and require minimal maintenance. They didn't mind even if the machines were bulky as it was for office purpose. All companies were making heavy copier machines for industry only at that time. However, challenging the industry logic, Canon created a Blue Ocean of new market space by shifting the target consumers of the copier industry from corporate purchasers to individual users. With their convenient and easy-to-use desktop copiers and printers, Canon created new market space in the industry.

The only way to beat the competition is to stop trying to beat the competition.

The Point of Difference	
Red Ocean	**Blue Ocean**
Compete in existing market space.	Create uncontested market space.
Beat the competition.	Make the competition irrelevant.
Exploit existing demand.	Create and capture new demand.
Make the value-cost trade-off.	Break the value-cost trade-off.

4.

BADGE ENGINEERING

"The essence of strategy is choosing what not to do".
- Michael Porter

Badge engineering is one such strategy which focuses essentially on doing few things only on your own and taking help of others for rest of the thing.

Ever wondered why the Toyota Glanza and Maruti Suzuki Baleno look so similar? Well, that's because they're exactly the same vehicle, but sold under two different brand names. This practice is called badge engineering or rebadging, which is the practice of applying a new badge to an existing vehicle and marketing and selling it as a different product or brand. (See the Table for other examples)

Rebadging is very common in highly capital-intensive industry like automobile industry as designing and manufacturing completely new car is very costly and time-consuming process. Besides, it is even more difficult to establish a new brand in the market. At times it takes several months before the brand gets recognition and becomes successful. However, it is comparatively less expensive for the manufacturers to re-badge a successful car and leverage its popularity. The most recent example of rebadging in India is of Toyota Glanza which is the badge version of original product Maruti Suzuki Baleno.

Manufacturers normally apply modifications only to badges and emblems; that's why it's popularly known as badge engineering or rebadging. But at times, they even carry out some minor styling updates. This may include cosmetic changes to head-lamps, tail-lamps or the fascias (decorative panels of a car's dashboard) to give the car a new look. In some cases, they may also offer different mechanical components such as the engine, transmission and safety features also.

The biggest risk with this strategy is that, if the marketing of badge engineered models goes wrong, these cars may not be able to carve out separate identities and could work against the manufacturer, as it would cannibalize sales of the donor model, or vice versa.

Badge Engineering in India Few examples			
Sr. No.	Car 1	Car 2	Country1, Country 2
1.	Suzuki Baleno	Toyota Glanza	India, India
2.	Fiat 124	Premier 118NE	Italy, India
3.	Morris Oxford III	Ambassador	UK, India
4.	Suzuki Alto	Maruti Alto	Japan, India
5.	Suzuki Fronte	Maruti 800	Japan, India
6.	Suzuki Swift	Maruti Swift	Japan, India
7.	Daewoo Matiz	Chevrolet Spark	Korea, India
8.	Skoda Rapid	Volkswagen Vento	Europe, India
9.	Suzuki SJ413	Maruti Gypsy	Japan, India
10.	Suzuki Splash	Maruti Suzuki Ritz	Japan, India

5.

UBER: REDEFINING THE CAR RENTAL INDUSTRY

Uber owns no vehicles, employs no drivers, and pays no vehicle maintenance costs. Still it has become one of the biggest companies in the world largely due to its ability to solve customer problem innovatively and user-friendly way.

Car rental industry is here for years. Uber has not created anything new but its ability to solve customer problems creatively, made it one of the leading companies in car rental industry. Uber has changed the way the world moves by seamlessly connecting riders to drivers and by bringing cities closer and more accessible for riders just with the help of a mobile app. It has opened many possibilities and opportunities both for riders and drivers. Today the San Francisco based company has around 15 million rides per day across the globe.

The biggest reason of success for Uber is its remarkably user-friendly service. To access Uber, customers simply had to download the app, create an account. When they are ready to summon a car, they simply open the app and pressed a button. The app displays available drivers in the nearby location, and usually responds within seconds that a driver is on its way.

Though Uber has become synonymous with taxi rental but the success was not overnight. Uber also faced many problems on the customer front but its ability to solve these problems creatively helped it grow rapidly. Let us see how Uber sorted out various challenges it faced in an innovative yet simple way.

The fear of unfamiliarity: Uber noticed that people were not comfortable to ride with the unknown driver. Uber came up with the idea in which people can see the profile and status of drivers before hiring the cab. Users can also see driver's past trips, and the ratings. By doing so Uber was able to instill confidence amongst the user and has broken the fear of unfamiliarity in people.

People were not able to get real-time notifications about the ride: Due to this, people were facing hurdles in their daily lives, for instance, reaching out to their offices or doctor appointments. Uber came with the feature in which people could check out driver's location after booking the cab and they also get real-time notifications about their rides in terms of arrival.

People were afraid to stick in traffic for long hours: One of the biggest challenges, users faced because of the lack of knowledge about the shortest routes and where they could meet less traffic. Uber came up with the idea in which Uber app only provides one of the shortest routes with less traffic area to Uber drivers.

Users wanted to go cashless in Taxi, too: The cashless payment system was introduced by Uber in order to help people who wanted to travel cashless.

There were many such problems but Uber came out with user friendly solution for each of these problems and as a result it could built the world's largest fleet of vehicles without owning a single one.

Uber Business Strategy in one line: User Convenience through Technological Innovation

6.

AMAZON DASH BUTTON: ORDER PROCESS INNOVATION

The tiny stick-on buttons from Amazon allowed customers to quickly reorder popular household items with a press without opening the computer or even smart phone.

On March 2015, Amazon launched dash button. The customers now can order any products to Amazon by only pressing the button without even touching their computer or Smartphone. Push a button, order potato chips. Push another, order diapers, stick a Tide button to your washing machine and instantly reorder detergent when you run out. Now nobody needs to go through tedious web browsing every time they want to put an order. Amazon did process innovation by this $5 plastic button with a battery and WiFi connection inside. It made the order process much easier. By 2017, Amazon had over 300 buttons, partners were receiving half their Amazon orders via the Dash and it was available in more than 8 countries.

Amazon further simplified it by launching "Virtual" dash buttons. Virtual dash buttons are the same push-button, but digitized and tucked into Amazon's app. The virtual push buttons got immense success, so in early 2019 Amazon stopped selling original physical dash buttons.

The launch of the Amazon Dash was a phenomenal way to address customers' concern and created a smarter supply chain to simplify a customer's purchasing decision.

7.

NETFLIX REDEFINING MOVIE VIEWING EXPERIENCE THROUGH DISRUPTIVE INNOVATION

Netflix is an inspirational example of a company that successfully shifted their business model multiple times and grew exponentially because of that.

Netflix is an American technology and media services provider and Production Company headquartered in Los Gatos, California. It was founded in 1997 by Reed Hastings and Marc Randolph. Today Company's primary business is its subscription-based online streaming (OTT) service which offers online streaming of a library of films and television series, including those produced in-house. As of April 2020, Netflix had over 193 million paid subscriptions worldwide, including 73 million in the United States alone.

The first business of Netflix was to let people rent videos by selecting it online and having it delivered to their door. This service was unparalleled at that time and a big shift in the industry. A year later, Netflix introduced a subscription model, where customers could rent DVDs online for a fixed fee per month. The idea of business occurred when Reed Hasting (One of the founders of Netflix) ended up paying $40 extra for returning rental movie after the due date.

Netflix expanded its business in 2007 with the introduction of streaming media while retaining the DVD and Blu-ray rental service. The company expanded internationally in 2010 with streaming available in Canada, followed by Latin America and the Caribbean. Netflix entered the content-production industry in 2012 with its first series Lilyhammer. Netflix has greatly expanded the production and distribution of both film and television series since 2012, and offers a variety of "Netflix Original" content through its online library. By January 2016, Netflix was operating in more than 190 countries. In 2016 Netflix achieved a unique landmark by releasing 126 original series and films, more than any other network or cable channel.

Netflix net worth has already touched to $100 Bn in less than twenty years of its inception by just following some basic rules like;

- Consistently doing the obvious.
- Producing its own content to reduce dependency.
- Continuously innovating and updating but still focusing on the same need of customer that is movie watching.

- Providing free trial for experiment to the customer which is a must when you are doing something completely new.

Because Netflix is offering a great product that customers wanted, people are willing to pay a little extra also compare to its newly evolved competitors like Amazon Prime Video.

One of Reed's inspirations for Netflix came from the gym he belonged to. He observed that the gym only had to attract a customer once, but it could continue to charge customer's every month. He quickly learned that as long as the business is giving the customer something they want, subscription-based buyers will stay on board.

8.

FACEBOOK'S ACQUISITION OF INSTAGRAM; STRATEGY TO CORNERING A FLEDGLING MARKET

One very common business strategy for larger firms to gain a stronghold in a growing market is through aggressive Merger and Acquisition strategy i.e. to buy out a competitor. These strategies not only give quick access to a new business but more importantly it kills the potential competitors. This obviously results in profit and expansion at large scale.

In April 2012, Facebook changed the mobile startup scene overnight by acquiring the photo sharing startup, Instagram, for an unprecedented price of $1B. Many industry observers felt that Facebook paid unreasonably high price for just a startup which was yet to prove its mettle. Keep in mind that until then, Instagram had just 30 Million users and did not have an established presence on the Android Operating System. This looked like a rash decision from Facebook. But to everybody's surprise in just 2 years of acquisition (2014) Instagram's user base shot past to 150M and further reached to 600 Million in the year 2017. It became dominant photo sharing app on all mobile platforms. More importantly, it attracts the adolescents and teens that were leaving Facebook. The Strategy to acquire Instagram proved a master stroke for Facebook in more than one way; which can be understood by following facts.

- Instagram allows Facebook to compete in a market where it didn't have a very strong presence, and helps it retain younger users.
- By buying Instagram, Facebook ensured that it has a competitive advantage over Google, Microsoft, and other competitors.
- The acquisition of Instagram; photo-sharing app improved Facebook's position substantially at a time when industry expert started believing that Facebook is having a midlife crisis and isn't cool anymore.
- It was believed at that time that the future was on mobile devices. With Instagram, Facebook got to improve its mobile presence; an area that was seen as its weakness for the sprawling social network.
- Instagram now generates almost one out of every four dollars of Facebook's annual ad revenue.

In the end, the purchase of Instagram has proven to be a far more visionary transaction for Facebook.

Facebook's strategy in acquiring Instagram was to corner the fledgling mobile image sharing market, and hedges its bets for future growth. The $1B price tag may have looked excessive in 2012, but looks almost cheap today.

9.

THE TOYOTA WAY: THE STORY OF BEATING THE BIG THREE OF USA IN THEIR OWN BACKYARD

Way back in the year 1973, the 'Big Three' car makers in the USA (A reference to the three largest automobile manufacturers in North America: General Motors, Chrysler and Ford.) had over 82% of the market share. Today they have less than 50%. The main reason for this is the aggressive (and unexpected) entry of Japanese car makers, led by Toyota into the US market in the 1970's.

US market was so surprised when Toyota started selling Japanese-made cars in the US, at a price far lower than they could match. The car industry was a huge contributor to the US economy, so one of the first reactions from the government was to implement protective tariff (taxes) on all imports of cars thus making Japanese cars as expensive as locally made cars.

But the tactic failed as within few years, Toyota and many other Japanese car makers managed to establish their production plants on US soil, thus eliminating the need to pay any of the hefty import taxes. At first, US car makers weren't all that worried assuming that by moving production to the US, the production costs for the Japanese car makers would rise up to be roughly the same as those of the local car makers. But that didn't happen. Toyota continued to output cars on US soil significantly cheaper than US companies could. Their finely honed production processes were so efficient and lean that they were able to beat US car makers at their own game by focusing on the notion of 'continuous improvement'. They knew that the US car industry was more advanced and more efficient than the Japanese one. Toyota spent years studying the production lines of American car makers such as Ford and tried to copy what they did so well. They blended these processes with the strengths of their own, and came up with something even better.

Toyota proved that knowing your own weaknesses can be the key to success and one of the best business strategies you can ever deploy.

10.

'CHAI CALLING': ENGINEERING-BACKGROUND 'CHAI-WALLAS' ARE MAKING CRORES VIA THEIR DESI START-UP

In India, tea is not just a morning beverage to instantly wake your drowsy self, but is a way of life for many.

Making a cup of tea is not just an art now, but has turned into a startup venture in India. A tea stall named "Chai Calling" is creating a lot of buzz because of its unique feature of 'home delivery' of tea. This tea stall is all set to expand by creating tea-based beverage chain.

The journey started when two engineers Abhinav an electrical engineer and Parmeet a software engineer started a venture called "Chai Calling". Both were working as professionals in top MNCs with good package but the entrepreneur in them motivated them to do something different, and "Chai Calling" was born in the year 2014. Initially they started a tea stall near a metro station in Noida, named "Chai Calling" which received a normal response at the start but very soon it became famous. In no time they had three outlets in Noida and six outlets in Bareilly selling tea with some snacks.

They got the idea of business during their office time where they didn't like the machine tea so they used to go to the tea stall outside their office. They were not happy with unhygienic and unhealthy conditions of the Chaiwalas. This made them think that something could be achieved in this sector also. The strong desire to innovate motivated them to quit their jobs and decided to start their own tea stall business. They put their savings of Rs one lakh each into preparing the stall and also created a website and named the business "Chai Calling".

With some hard work, their turnover grew to over Rs 1 crores in no time and they created job for 35 people in very short period of time. Faster delivery was the key to success and Chai Calling's USP too; to ensure this they gathered a team of delivery boy known as Chai Brigade who are smart and fast enough to deliver orders within 15 minutes. The outlets serve more than 15 varieties of tea including green tea, lemon tea, black tea and ice tea. Though Chai Calling is becoming a brand, the prices are still pocket-friendly.

Inspired by the success of the business idea they are planning to expand their business with increased number of outlets in other cities in coming years. The founders believe that if there could be a coffee chain, pizza chain, then why not a tea chain.

With absolutely minimum investment and outstanding earning, the duo has left everyone surprised and certainly inspired many. The success of this startup has once again proved that to succeed you require innovative idea more than anything else.

11.

DABBAWALAS OF MUMBAI: THE ORIGINAL FOOD DELIVERY NETWORK IN INDIA

Dabbawalas are efficiently delivering the home-made lunchboxes to the people of Mumbai with precision even without any technology for more than 125 years.

You can't eat what's served in the restaurants on daily basis because of hygiene reason (and also because of cost). This is the reason why office goers especially the middle class prefer their own food at work place also, cooked in a way that don't upset their stomach. This gave rise to very unique business idea of delivering homemade food at workplace. The Dabbawalas as they are famously known as deliver the home-made lunchboxes to these people of Mumbai.

Everyday large number of people living in Mumbai gets ready for their office and leaves their house to reach their workplace from one part of the city to another in crowded trains or buses. Meanwhile, the housewives get busy putting together a delicious and healthy meal for their better halves. Here enter the Dabbawalas; the men, who are engaged in the job of collecting, organising, and transporting these Dabbas between homes and offices. The lunchboxes are picked up in the morning, delivered at offices predominantly using bicycles and trains, and returned empty in the afternoon at home.

This business of delivering tiffin boxes started in 1890, when the Parsi and British communities living in Mumbai were in the need of convenient tiffin delivery service. Mahadeo Bhavaji Bachche was the first dabbawala to start tiffin delivery service to a British man. Subsequently the demand for tiffin box increased from all quarters and the unique chain of Dabbawalas was born. Today there are over 5000 Dabbawalas, who deliver more than 200,000 lunchboxes on daily basis. They work 52 weeks of a year.

They have to be on their toes always as they get only 40 seconds to load and unload these boxes at the local stations; at some stations, this time is as less as 20 seconds only. The Dabbawalas are not highly educated therefore the whole system depends on symbols, signs, and colours for coordination and delivery of lunch boxes. For example, an abbreviation is used for the pickup point of the lunchbox, color coding is used for starting stations, numbers are assigned for destination stations, and markings are used for the dabbawala who is supposed to handle and deliver the lunchbox to the final destination. A single Dabba goes through six Dabbawalas before it reaches the consumer, still only one in every six million meals misses its destination. This precision has made "The Dabbawalas"; a unique case study for many B schools like Harvard and Stanford, which actually teach this case study as a part of their management studies curriculum.

People often get surprised to know how much does this time saving exercise cost to an individual customer? It is as low as 450 rs per month only. On the other end, each dabbawala is self-employed and earned around 8,000 rupees a month. It's seen as a job for life, where the workers live by the philosophy, "Anna Daan is Maha Daan", translating to donating food is the best charity.

These Dabbawalas are the men on whom lakhs of people in Mumbai rely on. It is safe to say that the Dabbawalas with the local trains are the two lifelines of Mumbaikars.

12.

FEDEX: THE OVERNIGHT DELIVERY SERVICE WAS ANYTHING BUT AN OVERNIGHT SUCCESS

FedEx Corporation is an American multinational courier delivery Services Company headquartered in Memphis, Tennessee. The name "FedEx" is a syllabic abbreviation of the name of the company's original air division, Federal Express, which was used from 1973 until 2000. The company is known for its overnight shipping service and pioneering a system that could track packages and provide real-time updates on package location (to help in finding lost packages), a feature that has now been implemented by most other carrier services also. Today, FedEx is the world's largest express transportation company which moves more than 3 million items to more than 190 countries each business day.

FedEx has built a massively successful business by consistently delivering on promises, but the journey hasn't always been easy. The founder and CEO Fred Smith had to overcome some serious obstacles on his way to become one of the most successful companies of 20th century.

Smith developed the business idea when he was just a college student. He was an undergraduate at Yale University in 1965. As a part of the coursework, he wrote an economics paper exploring the process of transportation based on his observation about how the shippers relied on transporting large packages across the United States by means of truck or passenger airplanes. Smith thought of a more efficient transportation idea. He wrote a paper on how a company carrying small, essential items by plane could be a much better business. However, his paper didn't get much appreciation from his teacher and was graded "C".

Smith did not give up on the idea and launched the company; Federal Express in 1971 with a $4 million inheritance from his father and $91 million of venture capital. Federal Express started air operations from the Memphis airport on April 17, 1973, with 14 Dassault Falcon 20 jet aircraft to move packages between 25 cities.

The first three years of operation saw the company lose money despite being the highly financed new company in U.S. history in terms of venture capital. It was not until 1976 that the company saw its first profit of $3.6 million based on handling 19,000 packages a day. Its fortune further changed after the deregulation of the airline industry in 1977. The young company was now able to purchase large jet aircraft to increase the number of packages that could be transported per day. Federal Express bought seven Boeing 727 aircraft shortly after deregulation, followed by the purchase of Boeing 737 aircraft. This helped company increased its profit in 1977. Very soon the company had 31,000 regular customers, including IBM and the U.S. Air Force, which used Federal Express to ship spare parts. Federal Express became a public company in 1978 to raise capital for further expansion. The year after going public the company made a profit of $21.4 million with 65,000 packages a day to 89 cities across the United States.

By the 1980s, FedEx became well established company. In the year 1983, it reported $1 billion in revenue, making it as the first company in American business history to reach this financial hallmark inside 10 years of startup without mergers or acquisitions.

Started with 14 planes and a team of 389 staff, now FedEx has more than 425,000 employees and 411 aircrafts. The revenue of FedEx in the year 2019 was $70 bn.

Fleet of FedEx

13.

ROLEX OYSTER: A CROWN WORTH FOR EVERY ACHIEVEMENT

Although the wristwatch is taken for granted nowadays, a century ago pocket watches were the norm. Much of the credit for this goes to Rolex and its founder Hand Wilsdorf who in 1905 noticed a shift in lifestyle and dress codes of people. The 24-year-old Wilsdorf perceived that wristwatches would soon eclipse the appeal of pocket watches to become an everyday necessity. So, Rolex began laying the groundwork for buyers to see their watches as a viable option for everyday wear, extreme activities, and everything in between.

No other watchmaker in the world commands this level of recognition or manufactures a product that's viewed as a tangible symbol of success as Rolex does. So how did Rolex build this remarkable reputation? Through a powerful combination of extraordinary design, unparallel quality, and of course, marketing genius.

The story of Rolex is intimately associated with human achievement. Hans Wilsdorf, the company's founder, saw the mutual benefit of equipping people who were record breakers with an Oyster watch and started looking for an opportunity for the same.

In 1927, they had a stroke of marketing genius when they kicked off a longstanding history of working with exceptional athletes and personalities. That year, Wilsdorf approached a young female marathon swimmer and solicit her help in demonstrating the waterproof qualities of the new Oyster watch. She spent 10 hours swimming in the cold English Channel wearing Rolex Oyster. This gave huge publicity to Rolex when leading newspaper published a front-page ad that promoted both the athlete's remarkable swim and the Oyster's superior water resistance.

History was repeated in 1953 when one of the biggest achievements in mankind history happened. It was the year when Sir Edmund Hilary with Tenzing Norgay became the first explorers to reach the summit of Mount Everest, the highest point on earth (29,035 feet above sea level). They also were equipped with the Oyster Perpetual Watches, once again giving Rolex Oyster a huge publicity. This feat was celebrated with the creation of the Oyster Perpetual Explorer an iconic timepiece till today.

Today Rolex Oyster is regarded as one of the most important inventions of recent years which over time has become the primary choice for explorers and pioneers of all types, thereby reinforcing the image of Rolex as Superlative watchmakers.

It is one thing to claim a watch is waterproof. It is quite another to prove it. Rolex did it exceptionally well at this.

14.

LENSKART: THE JOURNEY TOWARDS BECOMING THE LARGEST ONLINE EYE WEAR STORE IN INDIA

The business of eyewear is very profitable with margins as high as 500 percent. Launching such a lucrative business on a large scale through technology is truly revolutionary.

Lenskart is the largest online e-commerce site dealing in lenses, eyeglasses, sunglasses and other allied services. It was founded by Peyush Bansal in November 2010. Peyush after finishing his graduation from the MC gill university in Canada, and doing masters in entrepreneurship from IIM Bangalore started working for Microsoft. Later he decided to enter in an online business of eyewear which was still untouched largely due to its complex nature.

Lenskart's Journey towards becoming the largest online seller of eyewear was very challenging due to the mindset of people regarding buying of eye wear online but the vigorous marketing strategy brought the change and people started buying eyewear online.

Lenskart works in a very simple yet creative way to solve customer's problem. Assume that you are ordering your glasses online; Lenskart offers glasses in 3 sizes of small, medium and large. Even if you do not have a prescription (in metro cities), Lenskart offers a home eye check-up service where a trained optometrist will be there to assist you. If you have second thoughts about the products you have ordered, the Lenskart customer care has a 14 day no question asked return policy.

Today Lenskart offers over 5000 frames and glasses and more than 45 kinds of high-quality lenses and everything else in eyewear categories. They are currently serving 4000 people a day and are looking at scaling it to 200,000 people a day in the coming years. To help in this effort they have a team of close to 1000 people which operates across verticals, which includes manufacturing, eye technicians, customer service, technology and logistics. With chain of more than 400 stores in India, it has become a dominant player in both online and offline market of eye wears and has become a brand worth more than 400 crores in less than a decade's time.

The biggest reason for this exponential growth can be attributed to hugely untapped Indian eyewear market. One third of India's total population needs spectacles today. The word 'need,' refers to people who have some or the other eye-related problem and out of these only 25% actually wear spectacles. Now, if we add up people who want to wear glasses as a fashion accessory (These categories of customers are interested in owning multiple eye wears to go with a variety of looks), then the numbers are just insane. The market was heavily fragmented with small shops leading the charge. Lenskart with its online optical shop business have created an entire new sector and dominates with hefty 70% market share.

Peysuh and his determination tells us that doesn't matter what challenges we face in life, there's always a way out if we can just hold on to the tide and keep striving to get on the top.

15.

REVITALIZING THE BRAND HARLEY DAVIDSON THROUGH BRAND COMMUNITY

In 1983, Harley-Davidson faced extinction. Twenty-five years later, the company boasted a top 50 global brand valued at $7.8 billion. Central to the company's turnaround, and to its subsequent success, was Harley's commitment to building a brand community: a group of ardent consumers organized around the lifestyle, activities, and ethos of the brand.

Harvard Business Review, April 2009

Harley-Davidson, Inc., H-D, or Harley, is an American motorcycle manufacturer founded in 1903 in Milwaukee, Wisconsin. It is one of the major American motorcycle manufacturers to survive the Great Depression, numerous ownership and subsidiary arrangements, periods of poor economic health and product quality, and intense global competition to become one of the world's most iconic motorcycle brand widely known for its loyal following. Harley-Davidson brand revival story is very unique because it is one of the first brands to use brand communities for turnaround the situation. Back in the 1980s, amidst a declining American economy and increasing competition from the Japanese companies, life for this iconic brand became very difficult. Japanese companies were providing a similar quality product at a better price in comparison to Harley Davidson. Trouble further aggravated in 1982 when Harley Davidson was burdened with a debt of $90 million. Even after having a strong consumer base, the business was in havoc due to declining profit and hefty interest payments. At this stage, the company decided to invest in brand revitalization. The company learned the Japanese quality standards and control strategies and developed a better engine. This helped it to overcome all the quality issue faced by its consumers earlier. Now, it was time to reach out to its prospective as well as existing customers. But the company had a shortage of sufficient funds for advertising. It, therefore, adopted another tactic for promotion. It launched one of the first official brand communities, connecting its customers to one another. A "Harley Owners Group" was introduced for the Harley fans in the year 1983. HOG flourished as a sponsored club initiating community marketing. With this strategy, Harley-Davidson made a grand comeback in the business and became one of the most prestigious motorcycle brands in the world.

Harley Owner's Groups have been credited with saving the company from bankruptcy and being "the most successful community building effort ever engaged in by a company."

16.

HOW RATAN TATA BROUGHT LIFE TO FADING JAGUAR LAND ROVER

Ratan Tata, the chairman of the Indian conglomerate Tata Group faced 'humiliation' when he went to sell the group's fledgling car business to Ford in 1999. They were told "Why did you start this business when you do not know anything about it". The Ford representative said that they will do a favour by buying Tata's car division. Taking it on the chin Ratan Tata decided not to sale the car business and came back. Come 2008 and the same Ford's JLR brand were bought by Ratan Tata. Ford chairman Bill Ford thanked Tata, saying "you are doing us a big favour by buying JLR".

Ratan Tata bought Jaguar and Land Rover in all cash transaction of $2.3 billion from Ford in June 2008. Nearly half of what Ford Motor paid to acquire both brands few years back. Tata bought JLR at a time when it was going through a rough patch. The retro designs were getting outdated, and competing with new efficient diesel engines was just making the British car brand redundant. It's not that the American car manufacturer Ford did not tried the turnaround. The carmaker started the work much earlier with focus of resolving quality problems but, the carmaker failed to impress the luxury car market. Realising that it's not their cup of tea, Ford decided to sell it off.

Though Tata could buy JLR at relatively less price but the challenges were many and even bigger than they might have thought. Many analysts felt that the Tatas paid a very hefty price for a dying brand. Many even questions their ability to revive the brand as they themselves have not achieved much with their own brand "TATA Motors"? Problem further got aggravated when just few months after the deal was done one of the worst financial crises hit the world. It thrashed the auto industry so badly that some of the giants of auto world actually got closed down.

However, Ratan Tata was convinced that the new acquisition will turn out well in future; and he was right as in just few years the fortune of JLR started to change. Much of the credit for this goes to Ratan Tata himself as he took personal interest in reviving JLR brand. He travelled across the US to meet dealers and taking their feedback on Jaguar Land Rover brand to make it more contemporary. Tata identified three major areas for improvement; liquidity, cost control and new products. Company decided to invest more in R&D to revive the brand. They invested almost 14% of its annual revenues in R&D, much higher than the industry standards of 5%. The focus was on making new models more fuel efficient to make it more competitive. The XF and XJ sedans got more efficient engines in no time.

In 2013, the strategy to invest in new products started paying off and the company clocked 77,000 sales that year. It reached to 178,601 (almost three times in comparison to 2009) units in 2017 and with this the JLR revenue topped at $34 billion.

People who were saying that Tatas were making an expensive mistake were pleasantly surprised seeing the successful turnaround of JLR brand.

The story is even more remarkable because Tata has done what very few companies from emerging markets have been able to do i.e. to turn around and successfully run a troubled Western Company.

17.

HOW CANON BEAT XEROX BY USING THE NEW LANCHESTER STRATEGY

The most important aspect of the Lanchester Strategy is the need for concentration. In most cases, this means splitting your much larger opponent's force into pieces and then taking on each piece separately. Canon used this strategy very smartly to leapfrog the mighty Xerox.

Japan's Canon has come a long way since its days as a manufacturer of cheap cameras. Canon with its unique strategy went on to beat mighty office equipment rival, Xerox, in photocopier market and then by teaming up with Hewlett-Packard in the desktop printer business also.

The Japanese multinational corporation Canon smartly used Lanchester strategy (very common in military) in their conquest of Xerox for the lucrative photocopier market in the U.K. Canon got a foothold in the market by first concentrating its resources in Scotland. After achieving a 40% market share there, Canon then began to attack selected and tightly defined regions in England. At the same time, Canon began to invest more and more in both product development (in order to differentiate their product) and in expanding their marketing and sales staff. By the time Canon began their final push into the lucrative London market, they had a superior product and a numerically superior sales force. Rank Xerox (subsidiary of Xerox in UK) didn't stand a chance by the time they realized what was happening.

Canon was challenging a seemingly invincible monopoly of Xerox, as Xerox had invented the photocopier and had walled off its creation with a ring of patents. But still Canon persevered, largely because of indifferent attitude of Xerox towards change. Canon's head of research Ichiro Endo once said that that "Xerox had been making so much money on its copiers for such a long time that they were no longer hungry. Canon took advantage of this by constantly challenging Xerox.

Initial success for canon largely by beating Xerox on price. The real innovation came very late. It wasn't until 1970 that Canon brought out a copier based on its own technology. It was only in 1982 that it introduced a fast, compact, dry toner copier that could compete with Xerox machines head on. Canon also benefited with its low-cost, low-risk strategy of selling through resellers and dealers rather than building up a huge direct sales force like Xerox. It worked closely with its Japanese competitor Ricoh, and captured the low end of the copier market.

Very soon Canon beat Xerox in PC market also by bringing a sort of revolution in the PC market. Recognizing that the PC would require a small printer on the desk rather than a big one down the hall, Canon invented the laser printer. Again, it chose a low-risk way to introduce its product into Europe and America. In 1984 it teamed up with Hewlett-Packard wherein Canon would make the guts of the printer; HP would add the software and sell the box under its own label.

The essence of New Lanchester Strategy which canon followed is "Divide and Conquer". It's all about committing the maximum amount of your resources against the minimum amount of your enemy.

18.

THE END OF KODAK MOMENT: THE STORY OF HOW A LEGACY BRAND FAILED TO KEEP PACE WITH TECHNOLOGY

The way Photographs have been central part of our lives, Kodak was central part of photography for decades. But due to the rapid shift from film and paper to electronic images "Kodak" became just a "Moment" in history.

The story of a brand which was once synonymous with capturing stories with pictures ended when it filed for bankruptcy in 2012. Kodak also, like so many legacy brands have failed to keep pace with rapidly growing digital era and became irrelevant.

There was a time when Kodak was the king of the photography world. Kodachrome film captured the Kennedy assassination and also the first man on Everest. The phrase "Kodak moment" was so ingrained in the lexicon that it's still around today, long after the sun has set on film photography. The practice of making and sharing images is still alive but in the form of digital photography where Kodak do not stand a chance.

Kodak's executives didn't realize that the world around them was changing. They thought they know who was taking photos and why. Kodak thought that the way people shared and displayed photos was with hard prints, and that digital could never match the print quality of film photography. They were partially correct also as digital photos were low quality, both in color and resolution, and thus no match for film. But digital photography evolved with time and with it the way people took and shared photos also, making life difficult for Kodak

Kodak wasn't actually late-comer to digital photography; in fact, they only invented it. Their engineers created boxy prototype of it as early as in 1975, calling the technology "filmless photography". In 1991, they partnered with Nikon to market a professional grade digital camera, and in 1996, they debuted their first point and shoot. Still, compared to competitors such as Fuji and Olympus, Kodak moved slowly, choosing instead to focus on its core business of making and selling analog camera film; which paved the way towards closer.

Traditionally photography was the purview of dedicated, serious photographers only but with self-contained film cartridges like those that Kodak provided, photography became easy, something anyone could do. Digital took that to the next step, making cameras just another gadget. They were cheap to obtain, easy to use, and sold in electronics stores alongside other shiny toys. Suddenly Kodak was playing catch-up and realised that they no longer the rulers of the territory because the territory itself had moved.

Kodak is a sad story of potential lost. The American icon had the talent, money and even the future technology also but it lacked foresightedness to make the transition.

19.

MEESHO: THE INDIAN SOCIAL COMMERCE SITE WHICH ATTRACTED FACEBOOK

Meesho bridged the gap between sellers and buyers on popular social media platforms like Facebook, Instagram and WhatsApp with zero investment.

Meesho (means 'my shop') is an Indian origin social commerce platform founded by IIT Delhi graduates Vidit Aatrey and Sanjeev Barnwal in December 2015. This Bengaluru based startup is part of the rapidly growing market that is being termed as "social commerce industry". Most of the people benefitting from this industry are small time resellers who operate their businesses mostly from their homes.

Meesho business model is unique in many ways; which made it an instant success. **Firstly,** Meesho targeted women, predominantly the housewives. It was a risk which paid off; as the internet users in India were predominantly men (approximately 70%). Later on, it started targeting students also. Today nearly one-third sellers of Meesho are students. **Secondly**, Meesho has most of its customers in smaller cities and towns which are usually touted as the next frontline regions in India's quest for rapid economic development. These two things got Facebook's attention also and in June 2019 Meesho became India's first startup to receive investment from Facebook.

Over a period of time Meesho not only raised good funding but also earned many prestigious awards. Within first four years itself this startup claims to have a network of more than 2 million resellers who largely deal with apparel, home appliances and electronics items.

Meesho has successfully created an alternate distribution channel by empowering housewives, young mothers, aspiring entrepreneurs and students to launch, build, and promote their online business without any investment; a problem that most people, who want to start a business face.

20.

THE NEW COKE: HOW IT BECAME THE BIGGEST STRATEGIC BLUNDER IN CONSUMER GOODS INDUSTRY

April 23, 1985, was the day when Coca-Cola Company took arguably the biggest risk in consumer goods history when it completely withdrew their flagship product and replaced it with a "new" Coke in the US and some international markets. The new product is often referred to as "New Coke".

The product (New Coke) was developed and launched after years of R&D and taste testing and focus groups studies with consumers. They tested the New Coke formula on 200,000 subjects. The new flavor outperformed both traditional Coke and Pepsi in taste tests. Therefore, when it was finally launched in 1985, the company had enough confidence to simultaneously end traditional Coke production.

Mr. Goizueta the then chairman and CEO characterized the "new Coke" decision as a prime example of "taking intelligent risks". But the ground reality was all different. Within a few days of traditional Coke being withdrawn and replaced by "New Coke", backlash from consumers and the media started. For many consumers Coke was a cultural icon and they were angry that it was no longer available. Some people got depressed over the loss of their favorite soft drink. Many consumers in panic started filling their basements with cases of Coke. A man in San Antonio, Texas, drove to a local bottler and bought $1,000 worth of Coca-Cola.

Things were getting worst with every day passing. By June 1985, Coca-Cola Company was getting 1,500 calls a day on its consumer hotline, compared with 400 a day before launch of New Coke complaining about the decision to withdraw original coke. People started blaming Mr. Goizueta for this poor decision. Mr. Goizueta received a letter asking for his autograph saying, in years to come, the signature of "one of the dumbest executives in American business history" would be worth a fortune.

As a result, within 80 days company had to bring back the traditional coke. In July 1985 it returned to store as Coca-Cola classic. Now Coca-Cola classic was being sold alongside Coca-Cola ("new Coke"). The two brands had distinct advertising campaigns also to differentiate them. But all this was short lived; as the New Coke was subsequently withdrawn from the US market.

Though return of Coca-Cola Classic improved the sales but the company became a big, corporate joke. Poor Market research was the biggest reason which contributed to this debacle. **First;** Researcher failed to understand that though most people loved New Coke (in blind test) but not as the replacement of traditional coke. If respondent had known that in choosing New Coke, they would effectively be pulling old Coke from the shelves; their response could have been completely different. **Second;** Researchers failed to grasp that, Coca Cola also had symbolic significance to buyers, particularly in the American market. For this group that prefers tradition over novelty, New Coke couldn't hold a candle of continuity and familiarity of old Coke.

This debacle taught few important lessons. First, the customer holds the cards for success of any company and Second, Market research isn't just a numbers game, it is more about capturing consumers' feeling and attitude toward the brand.

21.

THE TURNAROUND OF ROYAL ENFIELD BRAND

If you had spent Rs 55,000 to buy a Royal Enfield motorcycle in 2001, you would now have an old, rugged bike. But if you had invested the same Rs 55,000 in shares of Eicher Motors, the company that makes Enfield bikes, your investment will be worth Rs 3.53 crore now.

Enfield Cycle Company was established in England by two partners R.W. Smith and Albert Eadie, in early 1890s to manufacture bicycles and subsequently motorcycles in 1901 under the brand Royal Enfield. During the first and second world war, the company supplied motorcycles to the British army. Post-world war (in 1948) the company introduced the 350cc and 500 cc Royal Enfield Bullet bikes. In the year 1955, Enfield of India based in Madras bought the license for manufacturing the motorcycle in the country. The original company shut shop in England in 1970 post entry of Japanese bikes. But the bullet continues its run in Madras, making it the longest running motorcycle in the world.

The Indian brand also was on the verge of shut down in early 2000s, but in 2004 Mr. Siddhartha Lal (Son of Vikram Lal, the founder of Eicher Motors) took over as the COO of Eicher group and scripted an incredible turn around for the brand. At that time the group had a diverse spread of about 15 businesses including tractors, trucks, motorcycles, components, footwear and garments, but none of the business was a market leader. Siddhartha Lal decided that full weight would be put on behind Royal Enfield and the trucks business only; as a result, they withdrew from all other businesses.

He focused on Enfield first, leaving trucks for later. In 2005, the company was selling only about 25,000 bikes every year. It was felt that fixed cost would spread at around 100,000 bikes a year. Lal focused on improving engineering and quality of Enfield bikes. His efforts started bringing results as the product quality improved substantially. The sales also started growing and by 2010 the company was selling 50,000 bikes a year, but from three different platforms. This is when Lal decided to build all Enfield bikes on a single platform to maximize economies of scale. The Enfield Classic, launched from this single platform, caught the fancy of customers. By 2020 the sales reached to more than 50000 units a month from 50000 units a year in 2010.

This incredible brand revival was possible largely due to visionary leadership of Siddhartha Lal. The team under Lal decided that, mechanical changes made to modernize the bike shouldn't dilute the Brand identity. It was decided that the individuality, the rugged looks, the build, the head lamps, the petrol tank and the thump of the bike were to be retained at all costs. A modern Aluminum engine initially failed to replicate the signature vibrations and thump of the old engine but later the team was able to arrive at a thump which was 70% of the original. Production processes was also revamped to improve quality and slowly the tide turned for Royal Enfield.

Talking about the same Lal once said in his interview that he drew inspiration from global brands like the Mini Cooper and Porsche, both of which were very focused and conscious about not diluting the core DNA. He added that when he was a student in the 1990s in the UK, he observed that small cars were very poorly designed when compared to the mid-size and larger cars. Then came the Mini, which changed the paradigm and made small cars really fun to drive. That is how he also focused on making the Royal Enfield, a mid-weight motorcycles fun to drive, yet retaining its DNA.

It is a remarkable story of how a physical product was modernized without the brand losing any of its characteristics that gave it the iconic status.

22.

AIRBNB: THE JOURNEY TOWARDS BECOMING THE BIGGEST START UP OF 21ST CENTURY

Airbnb, Inc. is an American vacation rental online marketplace company based in San Francisco, California, United States. It offers arrangement for lodging, primarily homestays, or tourism experiences. The company does not own any of the real estate listings, nor does it host events; it acts as a broker, receiving commissions from each booking. The journey towards becoming the biggest startup of 21st century started in late 2007 in San Francisco when two youngsters Brian Chesky and Joe Gebbia have just moved from New York. Without employment, they were having trouble paying their rent and were looking for a way to earn some extra cash. They noticed that all hotel rooms in the city were booked as a local conference attracted a lot of visitors. The youngsters saw an opportunity. They bought a few airbeds and quickly put up a site called "Air Bed and Breakfast." The idea was to offer visitors a place in their apartment to sleep and breakfast in the morning. They charged $80 each a night; and the remarkable journey started. Soon after, Harvard graduate and technical architect

Nathan Blecharczyk also joined the team as the third co-founder. The following spring of 2008, Nathan Blecharczyk help them get Airbed & Breakfast off the ground and officially launched it around the Democratic National Convention in Denver where over 20,000 people were coming and hotels were not having enough rooms to accommodate them all. The idea was to cater to these people with air, bread and breakfast. The idea clicked and the Airbnb became and overnight success.

The success of Airbnb can be contributed to its ability to find a need gap in the way the hospitality industry. They noticed that Hotels charge a higher rate when there is a big event that boosts demand. As a result, either people pay more or so many even left out. Airbnb decided to fill this gap and absorb all this extra demand and a unique business model born.

Though the idea was very novel but there were many security risks associated with the model itself. The whole concept of staying with a complete stranger was fundamentally slightly intimidating for many. But to their surprise people themselves started sending their resumes and LinkedIn profiles to prove that they are not security risks. Seeing this very sophisticated crowd for stay their confidence was boosted and founder felt that they were on right track. Over a period of time the founders build in many novel mechanisms for ensuring trust between the parties.

Today Airbnb provides a platform for hosts to accommodate guests with short-term lodging and tourism-related activities. Guests can search for lodging using filters such as specific types of homes, such as bed and breakfasts, unique homes, and vacation homes and many more. Before booking, users must provide personal and payment information. Some hosts also require a copy of government issued identification before accepting a reservation. Guests can chat with hosts through a secure messaging system. Hosts provide prices and other details for their rental or event listings, such as the allowed number of guests, home type, rules, and amenities. Hosts and guests have the ability to leave reviews about the experience.

Till date Airbnb have already served more than 500 million guests across the globe in more than 81000 cities. To date the Airbnb hosts have earned more than $65 billion by hosting guests. Today on an average every day 2 million bookings are done on Airbnb. These numbers are more than enough to tell how remarkable the journey has been.

Airbnb is a classic example of disruptive innovation. Their service couldn't compete with the big hotel chains in terms

of amenities and other characteristics hotel guests are accustomed to, but they were able to offer a more personal experience and able to showcase the local culture instead at a very affordable price.

23.

SAYING TATA TO ZICA: THE CASE OF BRANDING GOING WRONG

What's there in name? Everything when it comes to branding. It was reaffirmed once again when Tata Motors dropped "Zica" name from their most ambitious car after "Zika" outbreak in 2016.

In early 2016, Tata Motors the famous Indian car manufacturing company was planning to launch its one of the most ambitious hatchbacks named "Zica". The car's acronym "Zica" was derived from "Zippy Car" but the word suddenly had a different meaning when "Zika" virus (accidently very similar to Zica) started surfacing in some part of Africa. Very soon it surpassed the World Health Organization's threshold for an 'international emergency'. As a result, Tata Company decided to drop "Zica" name from their car to avoid any troublesome association with the mosquito-borne virus Zika.

Subsequently, Tata Motors held a poll to choose the new name for the car. The company received more than 37,000 suggestions during this three-day activity and finalized

"Tiago" name instead of "Zica". Ever since then the Tiago has played a key role for Tata in establishing the company again in the passenger car segment with over 1.7 lakh Tiago were sold in just first 28 months only.

Tatas were fortunate because the 'Zika' problem aroused well before commercial launch of the car (though name was already announced and heavily promoted also) so they got sufficient time to rebrand it. But not every company is so fortunate. There are many examples where otherwise a good product failed just because of poor brand name.

To avoid any such negative association many companies started playing safe by picking a word that has a pre-existing, universal meaning (like say, Vistara, which means limitless expanse) or pick a word that doesn't have any meaning in the dictionary sense (like say, Pepsi, which is essentially an amalgamation of two syllables).

This incident is a lesson for all that branding is absolutely critical to a business because of the overall impact it makes on your company. It can change how people perceive your brand, it can drive new business and increase brand awareness. At the same time if not done properly it can be a disaster also.

Branding is not an exercise which you take so lightly. The Tatas might have realised this in a very hard way if the Zika pandemic would have occurred after product launch. If they would have done proper research before choosing brand name "Zica", they might have realised that there is something very similar (the Zika virus) already exists as it was first found way back in 1947.

24.

PEPSI BLUE: ONE OF THE BIGGEST FAILURE FOR PEPSICO

Although heavily promoted by PepsiCo, including advertisements by pop singer Britney Spears and in film promotion in movies like "The Italian Job", Pepsi Blue is widely seen as a commercial flop as sales remained low.

Pepsi Blue was introduced in 2002 to compete with Coca-Cola's "Vanilla Coke". The flavor of Pepsi Blue was described by Pepsi as "berry" and much more sugary and syrupy than regular cola. The flavor was the result of taste-testing over 100 flavors over a period of nine months. It was designed to attract teenage consumers with its bright blue color and unique flavor. Though heavily promoted across the countries it failed so miserably that within just two years of its launching it was withdrawn from most of the market.

To bring blue color it was tinted using Blue 1, a highly controversial coloring agent banned in numerous countries at that time as it was rumored to cause cancer. In India the blue color created all together a different problem. It looked too much like commercial kerosene sold in India which has a bluish tinge. It created even bigger controversy when a boy actually drank kerosene thinking it was Pepsi Blue and was admitted to hospital. So even though it was heavily promoted in India during cricket world cup 2003 it failed bring much for the company and subsequently withdrawn.

Many experts even felt that customers didn't like its sweeter taste and rejected it.

Pepsi Blue was unusual in many ways like its taste or the color, which ultimately attributed to the failure. The story of Pepsi Blue is lesson for all about how Market research also can go wrong.

25.

PEPSI NEXT: A SOFT DRINK FOR THE NEXT GENERATION

Pepsi Next was a mid-calorie drink which was designed to fill the gap between normal sugar cola drinks and diet colas.

Pepsi Next was launched by PepsiCo into the US market in February 2012, and later on, in various international markets. The new product was described as a mid-calorie cola beverage, having a mix of sugar and artificial sweeteners. It was designed to deliver a full cola taste with reduced calories. While filling the market gap between full sugar and diet soft drinks, PepsiCo indicated that its prime target market was lapsed cola drinkers (giving them a reason to return to the product category once again). PepsiCo was highly committed to Pepsi Next providing it with strong launch and management support. In fact, according to PepsiCo it was their most significant product launch for several years.

Pepsi Next was PepsiCo's fifth attempt at a mid-calorie beverage after four previous attempts which all were not so successful and later on were withdrawn. Then why a highly successful company like PepsiCo would frequently come back to a product concept that they had struggled with number of times. The biggest reason was that the US carbonated soft drink (CSD) market was continuously declining by around 90 million cases a year. These consumers developed an inclination for other beverage solutions, such as water, energy drinks and juices. One of the underlying factors driving this behavioral change was the preference that some consumers have developed for reduced sugar. Therefore, PepsiCo saw "Pepsi Next" as a viable low-sugar alternative to traditional soft drinks, and a product that could tap into consumer's emerging dietary needs and to generate sales from outside the traditional cola market and to win back lost cola consumers.

PepsiCo was confident about the success of Pepsi Next despite numerous failure similar products because they believe that the market was now more ready for this type of product; that is, Pepsi Next was the "right product at the right time".

Even though one of the biggest launches in Pepsi's history, Pepsi Next was discontinued in early 2015 due to not meeting company's expectation.

Pepsi Next failed because it was targeting everyone at the same time and no one in particular.

Pepsi's previous attempt in mid calorie beverage segment.	
Pepsi Light (1970s)	It was lemon-flavored and contained 70 calories as opposed to a normal Pepsi can at 150 calories.
Jake's Diet Cola (1980s)	It came in at a mere 15 calories, but did not leverage the Pepsi brand name.
Pepsi XL (mid-1990s)	Another 70-calorie formula. The X stood for 'excellent taste' and the L stood for 'less sugar'.
Pepsi Edge (2004)	It was marketed as a "mid-calorie cola" with half the sugar of its regular Pepsi.

26.

PAYTM PIONEERING THE E WALLET BUSINESS IN INDIA THROUGH INNOVATIVE STRATEGIES

When Modi government decided to make India digital after demonetization in 2016; Paytm was one of the companies who got benefitted by this move and registered an increased growth then onwards.

Paytm or **"Payment Through Mobile"** is India's largest payment, commerce, and e-wallet enterprise. It was launched in 2010 with an idea of cashless transactions. It is the pioneer and leader of QR based mobile payments in India. Over a period of time Paytm has transformed itself into one of Indian giants dealing in mobile payments, banking services, marketplace, gold, recharge and bill payments, serving millions of customers. According to official statistics, by the end of January 2018, the estimated Net worth of Paytm was 10$ billion.

The compelling reason behind rapid growth of Paytm is its unique model. Paytm don't charge their users directly rather it gives handsome cash back and other offers on almost everything.

Then the question arise is, how does Paytm make money? Paytm makes money from its advertising revenue model. Paytm permits advertisers to list their ads on Paytm websites and in turn Paytm charge them lump sum or annual subscription fees. Initially revenue was generated from mobile recharge services, where they charged nil from their users but earned commission from network operators. Similarly, they earn from other companies also when customers make bill payments through Paytm. Paytm also earns through commission charged from sellers for selling their products from Paytm mall. Paytm has also partnered with other financial institutions and banks to sell their products and services like insurance, investments, loans etc. along with its own product.

By giving cash back to existing customers Paytm ensures that the customer will come back in future also and sticks with Paytm and keep using its services. This brand loyalty is invaluable especially when customers acquisition cost is very high.

Another way by which Paytm makes money is through the cashback that get accumulated in customer's Paytm Wallet. It is also a source of income for Paytm. As per the RBI guidelines, the money deposited Paytm wallet is deposited by Paytm in an Escrow Account with a partner bank. This escrow account deposit fetches Paytm certain interest which is decided as per the contract between the bank and Paytm. Another benefit of not refunding your money and keeping it in your wallet is to ensure that you use this money for future transaction on Paytm only. Another Paytm income source is interest on advance payment for customers.

Through such innovative strategies Paytm has successfully brought a transformation in the way Indians makes payment i.e. from being dependent on the use of cash in daily dealings to making digital payments for such dealings.

In January 2018, Paytm took the market by surprise when it announced its foray into gaming, a move unheard of then. The company reacted to it saying that adding gaming was not just attracts users, but also to increases the time they spent on the app. Ideas was to make something available so they can keep coming back.

27.

AMAZON REDEFINING ONLINE RETAILING WITH AMAZON PRIME MEMBERSHIP

Before 1994, shoppers had to travel to stores to discover and buy things. Shopping used to be hard work; wandering down multiple aisles in search of a desired item, dealing with crying and nagging kids, and waiting in long checkout lines. Today, stores try to reach out to shoppers anywhere, anytime and through multiple channels and devices.

On July 5, 1994, a company was named after the world's largest river 'Amazon'. In the course of a single generation, Amazon has grown from fledgling online bookseller to one of the most valuable and powerful corporations in the modern history truly justifying its name based on the largest river.

In its way towards becoming the largest retailing brand in the world Amazon has reshaped retailing industry permanently by bringing innovations one after another. Amazon continually took shopping convenience to newer levels through features like one-click ordering; personalized recommendations and ordering products with the single touch of a Dash button and many more. But one of the biggest changes brought by Amazon is its privilege service called "Amazon Prime".

In the year 2005 Amazon started this privileged service called Amazon Prime, as a two-day shipping membership (Paid membership) for devoted Amazon shoppers. Ever since then service has evolved to include many additional perks including a Prime credit card with 5 percent cash back. Perhaps the most prominent Prime perk, is access to Amazon Prime Video. The video on demand service started in 2006 as Amazon Unboxed, but was rebranded in 2008 and integrated into the Prime service three years later. It now boasts thousands of free TV shows, films, and games. Prime Music is another perk for Amazon Prime members. That means with the same annual fee, the members can enjoy unlimited music streaming as well. It offers more than a million music tracks or albums for streaming over the internet or download for offline listening without you having to purchase them outright.

Apart from these Amazon Prime offers many more benefits in a single subscription fee at just 999 Rs. per year (in India). Prime members get access to FREE in-game content like power-ups, exclusive collectibles, characters, outfits, skins, themes, in-game currency and more across popular mobile games, refreshed frequently. Eligible Prime members earn unlimited 5% reward points on all purchases on Amazon. in using the Amazon Pay ICICI Bank credit card. Members can enjoy Prime Reading on their Kindle E-reader, or install the free Kindle reading apps on mobile, tablet, PC or Mac. One can read as much as they want from hundreds of eligible eBooks. One of the biggest benefits to the Prime member is that you get access to exclusive deals across categories.

Success of Amazon Prime Membership can be understood with the fact that today about 100 million shoppers worldwide have Amazon Prime Membership.

Apart from Prime Membership, Amazon have brought so many innovations over a period of time that it started impacting other industries upto an extent that industry players and observers use the term "Amazoned" to describe their business model and operations being disrupted by Amazon. One such innovation is "Amazon Pay" for purchasing online goods elsewhere with your Amazon account. This program was aimed at developing markets such as India, which has a huge population that does not use banks. Amazon launched streaming device called Fire TV in 2014 to compete with Apple and other set-top box makers. The product has since been shrunk into a skinny HDMI stick known as Amazon Fire stick. With launch of Alexa, Amazon has one of the most pervasive digital voice assistants in the market today.

Today Amazon is not only the biggest retailer in the world but it is the most valuable companies in the world, with a market capitalization hovering around US$1.6 trillion.

Amazon is not only the world's largest online store, but it is much more than that. Today, Amazon is the largest tech employer by far. It employs more people than the next five tech companies combined. It has achieved this unique status by integrating large number of industries with unique and disruptive innovations.

28.

PARADIGM SHIFT IN HOTEL INDUSTRY DUE TO TECHNOLOGY

Twenty years ago, the only travelers that really understood the differences in the Hotel brands were frequent business travelers. Now with the availability of online ratings every consumer has the ability to research and compare properly various options available.

Over the past 20 years hotel industry has changed drastically. The ever-evolving technology has completely changed the way hotel business is conducted. As a result, consumers today have more services and amenities at lower, costs such as high-speed Wi-Fi, complimentary breakfast, expanded in-room technology and entertainment options, and fitness centers.

One of the biggest developments in the hotel industry is online hotel booking apps. Originally created to sell excess inventory during slow seasons, these online hotel booking apps have become one of the top drivers of hotel bookings around the world. Their customers range from both business and leisure travel. They have moved from offering simply hotel bookings to providing everything from language support to personalized experience suggestions and so on. There are many booking app which provides a lot of choices for bundling flights, trains, cars apart from hotel bookings. For example;

Pobyt is a hotel booking platform with a unique feature that allows you to book the hotel rooms on a per minute basis.

HotelQuickly is hotel booking app that allow the users to find the discounted hotel throughout the world. The service has access to over 450,000 hotels and is localized to 17 different languages. You can get additional discounts by referring your personal invitation code to your friends and relatives.

The Hotels.com allows user to save all their favorite hotels to easily compare between features and prices. You can see your past, current and future hotel bookings, even when you don't have access to the Internet.

Trivago claims to be the world's largest hotel search and information website which allows you to compare hotel prices accumulated from over 200 third party booking sites worldwide. This helps to save you the time and effort of visiting each one of these sites individually. It claims to have 45 million monthly users and a million searches per day.

Travelspice works on a concept of bidding. Customers bid a certain amount for a hotel room, which is expected to be cheaper than standard room rates and then Travel Spice works with several hotels in the area to check who is willing to offer a room to its guest at the bid price. Hotels with lots of empty rooms will be happy to grab whatever they can get and probably won't mind giving out a room at low price to the bidder. If multiple hotels bid, Travelspice assigns best of the hotel will be assigned to the customer.

The Online hotel booking system is actually improving the lifestyle and standards of the people by simplifying their decision-making process.

29.

CADBURY CELEBRATIONS - EATING INTO THE TRADITIONAL SWEETS MARKET THROUGH INNOVATIVE MARKETING STRATEGIES

One of the most exciting marketing strategies is spotting a market opportunity within a traditional product space and exploiting it. One such example is Cadbury Celebrations which through its clever marketing strategy made inroads into traditional sweet market of India.

Indians have a long and cherished tradition of gifting sweets on occasions, be it festivals, weddings, ceremonies, or any other celebrations whether personal or corporate. The category of 'gift sweets' is traditionally dominated by traditional Indian sweets like ladoo, Barfi, Rasgulla, sandesh etc. Traditional sweets occupy a special place in the Indian psyche and gifting them is considered auspicious (from their use as offerings to deities) and a gesture of goodwill. The process of choosing and buying sweets is considered very important because of the belief that sweets creates a special bonding and relationship.

As a result, this segment was traditionally dominated by traditional sweets only until Cadbury spotted an opportunity in this category also. Cadbury realised that despite having huge varieties, all Indian sweets eventually fell under the same title mithai (traditional sweet) and largely made from milk and milk made items only. Cadbury was quick to identify this gap (lack of alternatives) and decided to come out with something which is different from traditional sweets but still holds the Indian tradition.

As a result, Cadbury celebration was born as a premium chocolate pack. Designed as a "gifting product", Celebrations was launched in several assortments as a collection of Cadbury's traditional brands like Dairy Milk, Five Star, Perk and Gems, or in combinations of rich chocolate and exotic ingredients like almond, cashew and caramel. It was grand in presentation and fairly expensive to be considered for gifting.

While positioning and designing Marketing campaign for Celebrations, Cadbury realised that apart from being delicious, the traditional sweets were ingrained in Indian's culture. So, creating and projecting something as a superior alternative to Mithais was a risk. So, Cadbury positioned it (Celebrations) not as an alternative to mithai rather as an exciting "Gifting concept", one that people looking forward to receive. Since its launch in 1992, Celebrations is presented as a gifting choice when one really cares about the receiver and when one knows that expectations are higher than just a traditional mithai.

The campaigns for Cadbury Celebrations were all centered around emotion and sentiment. The TVCs consistently featured various occasions for gifting and sharing like Diwali, Raksha Bandhan etc. The focus was on relationships; be it brother and sister, friends or families. The idea was to showcase how relationships occupy a special place in our lives and how we can celebrate it with Cadbury Celebrations. The idea was to promote the magic of gifting and sharing and spreading happiness through gifting. Cadbury found and created different occasions which can be celebrated, and 'Cadbury celebrations' were there as a possible gift to celebrate these occasions.

Adoption of Cadbury Celebrations was swift and widespread. People accepted Celebrations as a respectable gifting option, one comparable to Indian sweets. The comparable price made the brand a remarkable success.

Cadbury has popularized, glamorized, and commercialized the idea of gifting and made it a source of happiness through a perfect blending of marketing and socio-cultural values.

30.

KIZASHI: A RARE FAILURE FOR MARUTI SUZUKI IN INDIA

Maruti Suzuki India Limited has been the leader in Indian car market ever since its inception in 1983. It is said that no car companies in the world knows Indian customers better than Maruti. So, when it fails it becomes a case study for all. One such rare failure for Maruti is failure of its most ambitious car "Kizashi", which failed so terribly in India that it was withdrawn within just two years of its launch.

Kizashi was a mid-size car manufactured by Japanese automaker Suzuki. **'Kizashi'** is a Japanese word which means "something great is coming". Kizashi was first unveiled in the United States on July 30, 2009 and subsequently launched in Japan, North America, Australia, New Zealand and European markets. Aspired to be Suzuki's flagship sedan Maruti Suzuki Kizashi was launched in India on 2nd February 2011 with priced at around 16 to 17.5 lakh rupees. It was an ambitious attempt from Maruti to enter in Indian premium sedan car segment as earlier attempts

(Grand Vitara and Baleno) to enter this segment were all disasters. So, desperate to make an inroad in this segment Maruti launched its most premium car "Kizashi" in 2011.

Though Kizashi had impressive looks and advanced features; still it flopped so badly that within 18 months the nationwide sales came down to just 10 units per month. This forced company to withdraw it from Indian market.

The failure of Kizashi made the company and industry expert wondering. How come a company who in a way defines the rule of the game in Indian market failed even after having produced an excellent car?

According to many company's Brand Image was the biggest reason for this failure. Maruti is known as car maker for middle class customer in India. It has always branded its cars as fuel efficient and low-cost car. Advertisements like "Petrol khatam hi nahi hota", "Kitna deti hai" exemplify this viewpoint. This image made the company market leader in India but the same image distanced the company from the premium buyers. As a result, whenever Maruti tried to impress the premium buyers it failed even after having made good quality cars; and Kizashi was no exception to that.

Another issue with Maruti was that it lacked snob value necessary for luxury segments. The premium buyers who pays premium price to buy a car are not merely looking for a swanky car with high end features. Part of the price premium that they are paying is just to get associated with a premium brand like Skoda, BMW, Mercedes, and Audi etc. Maruti is definitely not one of them. So even after having advanced set of features, buyers didn't accept Kizashi as a car worth of 17 lakh.

Distribution channel was also an issue. The car was available at all Maruti Suzuki showrooms; a spoilsport in providing the right kind of ambience for luxury car consumer. A premium buyer expects to be treated exclusively. However, in the case of Kizashi, a potential buyer had to visit the same Maruti showrooms that were flocked by consumers of low-priced cars like Alto or WagonR. The worst part was that the premium buyers were attended by the same personnel who attend a regular customer (Middle class customer) of Maruti. Even though personnel were warm and nice they were not trained to attend a luxury car consumer.

There was an issue on strategic front also. The company was not sure whether such type of product will succeed in Indian market or not. So, they decided to play safe by bringing Kizashi in CBU (Completely built unit) form, which means the whole car was made in Japan and loaded on a ship which then came to India. However, the distinct disadvantage of bringing the car in a CBU form was that it attracted import duty which ultimately increased the price substantially. As a result, Kizashi's top model priced at 17 lakhs in India against USD 25,000 (around 12-13 lakhs) in the US market (as it was manufactured in USA for USA market). This unreasonably high price further distanced the buyers from the brand.

Things could have been different for Kizashi if it was manufactured in India as it would have reduced price substantially.

A better way for Maruti would have been to launch an exclusive brand to attract the premium buyers and differentiate it from Maruti brand name, the way Toyota maintained two separate brands 'Toyota' and 'Lexus' for two different class of customers.

Almost every leading company in the world have adopted this approach to maintain the much-desired exclusivity for exclusive segments.

31.

THE END OF THE ROAD FOR INDIAN ICON "AMBASSADOR"

Hindustan Motor's iconic car 'Ambassador' became history in 2014 when the company decided to suspend its production due to continuous decline in sales. Despite the fact that it had over 70% market shares at one point of time; it could sale only 2200 cars in its last financial year against industry sales of more than 1.8 million.

Ambassador was launched in 1958 and for many years it was just about the only car available in India. People had to wait for months from the date of booking to get the delivery of Ambassador. Ambassador can be called as the first indigenous car of India as it was the first car to be produced in India; though the car owes its design and technology to a British car model Morris Oxford. The "Ambi" as it was popularly known as was famous for its sturdiness, round shape, space and comfortable seats. Owning an ambassador used to signify that the person is rich and powerful. The car was popular amongst all classes; let it be the bureaucrats, Zamindars, Corporate honchos or even the taxi drivers.

The Ambassador hugely got benefited by the restrictive business environment of India at that time. The licenceraj, red tapism and the unfriendly economic policies ensured that no other player entered Indian car market for years. This created an almost monopoly for Ambassador (and Fiat's Premier Padmini). The protected environment helped it grow rapidly but also made it complacent. As a result, throughout its life, Ambassador the product never changed sparing a few cosmetic changes.

The supremacy was first challenged in 1983 when Maruti Udyog Ltd (a joint venture between Government of India and Suzuki motors of Japan) launched its first car, Maruti 800. Ambassador's dominance began to slip and started losing its market leadership to Maruti; which began producing low-cost hatchbacks. Maruti got hold on the family segment (the largest car segment in India even today) in no time with its small, compact, fuel efficient and low maintenance cars.

Even after losing the bulk of the market to Maruti HM's Ambassador didn't change. As a result, when market was completely opened post liberalization it was impossible for Ambassador to survive against the superior global players. The competition was immense and the quality of cars has got altogether a new definition. Consumers now had new set of purchase considerations like quality, brand, driving comfort, luxury, and cost of maintenance etc. where Ambassador found it difficult to fit.

There was still some hope for Ambassador as it was the only car with diesel engine at that moment. But this advantage also soon vanished when Tata launched 'Indica' with diesel engine. The diesel loving consumers got better car with contemporary design against an outdated, old-fashioned Ambassador at an affordable price. The nail in the coffin came for Ambassador when Indica took away its taxi market also.

One of the biggest reasons for failure of Ambassador was its high price. In 2013/14 Ambassador's price was around Rs 480000. At that price people had options like Tata Indigo which was far more luxurious and contemporary. The HM plant achieved full depreciation in 2000 itself but they didn't pass it to customer by reducing the price and paid the price.

There were no significant changes in the design decade after decade and the new generations of customers didn't find it appealing.

Since the then prime minister Atal Bihari Vajpayee opted for a sleek custom-made BMW in 2003, it's been steadily downhill for the grand old lady that had once ruled Indian roads.

32.

FALL OF BAJAJ CHETAK: A CASE OF MARKETING MYOPIA

The image of an Indian family with the husband driving a Bajaj Chetak scooter, wife sitting at the back with two kids was too common for almost four decades.

Bajaj Chetak was launched in 1972 and was based on the design and specifications of Italian scooter company Vespa's Sprint model. The name Chetak was based on Maharana Pratap's horse which was legendary for its bravery and power. Chetak became an instant hit among the Indian middle class due to its reliability and sturdiness coupled with reasonable price and the low maintenance.

By 1977, Chetak raced ahead of every other player in the two and four-wheeler category securing sales of over 100,000 units a year. The waiting list was never ending and people used to pay extra to buy a Chetak. If reports are to be believed, Chetak was an unavoidable dowry at that time.

In the mid-1980s, Bajaj discontinued their partnership with Vespa, and started producing 100% Indian made Chetak scooters, which gave rise to their famous slogan: "Hamara Bajaj".

The brand started to lose its relevance in the post liberalized era. It failed to appeal the younger generation and the time ran out for "Hamara Bajaj" as Hero Honda and TVS Suzuki made the two-wheeler market motorcycle-led. Against vehicles returning 80 kmph, Bajaj scooters returning 40 kmph stood no chance.

The company also failed to understand the changing perception of the customers towards scooters. Scooters have become gearless by then and were no more family rides, but peppier individual modes of transport. Bajaj's inability to bring a gearless scooter made it outdated.

Bajaj had huge brand equity still it failed as it did nothing with the product for 40 years of its dominance. It had the same look, same quality and style throughout its life. The product had serious problems like starting trouble and riding comfort. The "Tilting the Chetak to the side for starting was a common joke. Bajaj never took this problem seriously and did nothing in product development. The R&D spent for a long time was a miniscule 1%. So, without addressing any product problems, how can you expect the customer to buy the product? The moment they got a better option they switched and the journey ended for Chetak.

Chetak was officially put to rest in the year 2009 when company decided to solely concentrate on its bike business in the changed market scenario.

Undisputed leadership often leads to indifference and ignorance. Bajaj went into a dormant state and failed to wake up to changing market dynamics until it was too late. Bajaj was never a leader in technology but they never bothered about it and paid the price.

33.

COCA COLA ACQUISITION OF THUMPS UP: A LESSON IN GLOBALIZATION

After fighting almost, a lone battle to stop the entry of America's cola giants into India, Ramesh Chauhan of Parle Agro finally gave up in 1993 and sold his major soft drinks brands Thums Up, Gold Spot and Limca to Coca Cola.

In 1977, Ramesh Chauhan along with brother Prakash Chauhan and then Parle CEO Bhanu Vakil launched Thums Up as their flagship beverage after the American company Coca-Cola withdrew from India, due to new regulations brought by government for foreign companies operating in India. Ever since its launch Thumps Up enjoyed huge success.

But things suddenly changed when Coca-Cola re-entered India in 1993, in its second stint. Parle decided to sell (forced to sell?) Thums Up, Limca and Gold Spot to Coca-Cola for around $60 million. Terming it a pure business decision, Chauhan said, we did not have much choice, because we were working through a typical franchise system which is not favourable to us. The franchising system entailed that each franchise partner was the owner of his own plant. Chauhan's hand was forced, since most franchises declared their intentions to team up with Coca-Cola. So, he decided to sell off soft drink business and concentrate on the bottled water business. The brand Bisleri was doing quite well and seemed to have a very bright future ahead due to huge untapped market.

Coca Cola also didn't have much option other than acquiring the market leader Thumps Up because of their late entry to Indian market. Coca Cola entered in 1993 (after liberalization) due to its bitter experience in their first stint in India, where they had to wind up their business overnight in 1977. Pepsi entered Indian market in 1988 (before liberalization), as a result it was an established player when coca cola entered. So, Coca Cola was struggling from the first day. In order to get a foothold in India, Coca Cola had 3 options:

1. Gradually expand operations by building its own plants throughout India. This process would have taken several years.
2. Poach bottlers (franchises) of other cola brands by offering them irresistible benefits.

3. Acquire a company which already has all the facilities in place, so that Coca Cola can reach out to every nook and corner of India from day one.

Coca Cola started with the 2nd option, i.e. Poaching bottlers. Although Parle was the market leader with more than 80% of the market-share catered by 62 bottlers across India, it was a fragile business model because Parle owned only 4 bottlers while the rest (58 bottlers) were owned by franchises. Most of these franchises were not happy with Ramesh Chauhan's autocratic leadership style and they were excited to work for foreign brands. Hence, it was very easy for Coca Cola to hunt down the top bottlers and poach them. Ramesh Chauhan was helpless because almost every week, there would be news of one more bottler switching to Coca Cola. If this would have continued, then Parle would have end up with less than 10 bottlers (since 4 were its own and few were still very loyal to it), thereby losing significant market share and dying a natural death.

By September 1993, Ramesh Chauhan realized that there was no point fighting with the giant which was on a poaching spree and decided to "surrender". It was a very tough decision to make because these brands (Thums Up, Limca, Gold Spot) were carefully nurtured by Chauhan like his own children and now he had to sell them off.

It was double-bonanza for coca cola because firstly, it managed to instantly reach out to every part of India, and secondly, there was no significant competition because the leader itself was acquired.

"It is a great feeling that Thums Up is still number one. Despite all the years gone by, these multinationals' own brands have not been able to overshadow Thums Up."

--Ramesh Chauhan

34.
TRAVELSPICE

It is well said that no business is free from internal hard time and external competition but it is also equally true that sky is the limit for those who innovates and experiments. Travelspice is one such company which with its unique business model became an instant hit in hotel industry.

Evolution of internet technology has changed the dynamics of many industries completely. Hotel industry is one such industry. Today customers have so many options while booking a hotel online. Traditionally a hotel customer used to pay on per day basis for a set of standard facilities like breakfast, clean room, toiletries, wifi etc. But due to competition, same hotel started to sell same room in many different ways; there's a rate without breakfast, there's a rate with both breakfast and dinner, some hotels have a night only rate (like 8PM to 8AM) or day only rate and so on. That's why today booking a hotel without knowing full list of what is included and what is not could result in you spending a lot extra than what you thought you will be paying.

There are so many companies who are in online hotel booking business such as Goibibo, MakeMyTrip. These companies through their innovative business strategies have redefined the hotel industry. One such company is Bangalore based TRAVELSPICE, who also won Travel tech startup of the year 2018 award from the Government of Karnataka. It was founded by Ramu Kallepalli, Prashant Mitta and Ankit Manglik in February, 2017 and within no time this online hotel booking app made it mark in more than 220 cities across India and 10 cities outside the country because of its innovative and unique business model.

TRAVELSPICE works on a concept of bidding. Customers bid a certain amount for a hotel room, which is expected to be cheaper than standard room rates and then it works with several hotels in the area to check who is willing to offer a room to its guest at the bid price. Hotels with lots of empty rooms will be happy to grab whatever they can get and probably won't mind giving out a room at low price to the bidder. If multiple hotels bid, Travelspice assigns best of the hotel to the customer. It works on two simple principles;

1. It maintains a floor price for each room category (1 star to 5 star) so that customers won't bid extreme low rates. Customers can only bid above this floor price.

2. TravelSpice offers a provision where you can exclude some hotels you don't like (Max 3) though this feature is available only when lots of choice is available, not when only 4 hotels are available for the selected category.

TravelSpice has an interesting revenue model; they don't take a specific commission for each transaction instead they take the difference in the amount of user bid and hotel bid. Thus, users get the value, hotels get customers and TravelSpice make money.

BIBLIOGRAPHY

https://timesofindia.indiatimes.com/blogs/WebWise/the-reason-why-nokia-and-blackberry-died/

https://www.theatlantic.com/business/archive/2013/09/why-nokia-died-nobody-buys-phones-anymore/279337/

https://studiousguy.com/blue-ocean-strategy-definition-and-examples/

https://www.drivespark.com/off-beat/badge-engineering-india-rebadged-indian-cars-010687.html

https://www.spaceotechnologies.com/uber-growth-strategy-lesson-startups-entrepreneurs/

https://www.businessmodelsinc.com/exponential-business-model/netflix/

https://en.wikipedia.org/wiki/Netflix

https://blog.udemy.com/business-strategy-examples/

https://www.executestrategy.net/blog/the-5-best-business-strategies-ive-ever-seen/

https://predictableprofits.com/fedex-still-thriving-can-learn-success/

http://www.dailytenminutes.com/2017/09/success-story-fred-smith-federal-express.html

https://www.thebalancesmb.com/federal-express-fedex-2221098

https://brandriddle.com/fedex-success-story/

https://digital.hbs.edu/platform-rctom/submission/fedex-the-worlds-largest-continuous-flow-process/

https://www.rolex.org/en/perpetual/making-history-with-rolex?ef_id=CjwKCAjw97P5BRBQEiwAGflV6ZdVaQK5jWtL8BvBqOhreNlhuwg2WkHQ9KGfdrZMbIPLRbEQuLdhOBoCXEsQAvD_BwE:G:s&s_kwcid=AL!141!3!395287334607!e!!g!!rolex%20story

https://musings.lemonture.com/lenskart-com-the-story-of-the-other-bansal-1743f06b8ee5

https://corporatebytes.in/success-journey-peyush-bansal-founder-lenskart/

https://auto.economictimes.indiatimes.com/news/passenger-vehicle/cars/how-ratan-tata-brings-life-to-jaguar-land-rover/63241719

https://customerthink.com/how_canon_used_the_new_lanchester_strategy_to_defeat_xerox/

https://www.forbes.com/forbes/2001/0723/068.html#314cb3f25f3e

https://info.madisontaylormarketing.com/blog/marketing-impossible-how-kodak-died

https://techcrunch.com/2019/06/13/facebook-meesho-first-indian-startup-investment/

http://www.yourtechstory.com/2019/09/30/meesho-india-first-facebook-backed-startup-emerged-out-failed-business/

https://www.business2community.com/consumer-marketing/market-research-fail-new-coke-became-worst-flub-time-01256904

https://www.greatideasforteachingmarketing.com/new-coke-case-study/

https://www.coca-colacompany.com/news/the-story-of-one-of-the-most-memorable-marketing-blunders-ever

https://economictimes.indiatimes.com/industry/auto/two-wheelers-three-wheelers/how-siddhartha-lal-turned-royal-enfield-into-a-global-brand/right-people-at-the-right-places/slideshow/61531001.cms

https://mpk732t22016clusterb.wordpress.com/2016/08/28/the-royal-enfield-bullet-reborn-from-the-ashes/

https://getpaidforyourpad.com/blog/the-airbnb-founder-story/

https://growthhackers.com/growth-studies/airbnb

http://www.greatideasforteachingmarketing.com/pepsi-next-case-study/

https://www.feedough.com/paytm-business-model-how-paytm-makes-money/#:~:text=million%20registered%20users.-,Business%20Model%20of%20Paytm,wallet%20and%20reservation%2Fbooking%20options

https://yourstory.com/2019/04/gaming-strategy-phonepe-paytm

https://www.weforum.org/agenda/2019/07/amazon-is-turning-25-here-s-a-look-back-at-how-it-changed-the-world

https://www.theverge.com/2018/10/23/17970466/amazon-prime-shopping-behavior-streaming-alexa-minimum-wage

https://yourstory.com/mystory/top-10-best-hotel-booking-apps-in-india-bwe8xn3jy0

https://www.thehindubusinessline.com/companies/no-regrets-selling-thums-up-says-bisleri-chief-ramesh-chauhan/article23106362.ece#

http://guruprasad.net/posts/part-13-thums-up-story-ramesh-chauhan-sells-parle-brands-coca-cola/

https://theinvestorsbook.com/brand-revitalization.html

https://hbr.org/2009/04/getting-brand-communities-right

http://marketerideas.blogspot.com/2011/07/cadbury-celebrations-eating-into.html#:~:text=Cadbury%20Celebrations%20%2D%20Eating%20Into%20the%20Traditional%20Sweets%20Market,-One%20of%20the&text=In%20fact%2C%20the%20psyche%20is,a%20special%20reason%20or%20relationship.

https://www.incuspaze.com/travelspicc-hotel-booking-2-0/

About the Author

Dr. Pratik C Patel has a rich teaching experience of around 14 years at UG and PG level. He has done his Ph.D in Celebrity Endorsement. He has also cleared NET in Management subject. He has published more than 25 research papers/ case studies in the journal of repute. He has already published two books titled "Contemporary issues in Marketing and Finance" and "Learning Business Strategy through Case Study".

Dr. Patel is presently associated with one of the most reputed Management College in the South Gujarat region, BRCM College of Business Administration; affiliated to VNSGU as Assistant Professor in the subject of Marketing Management since June 2009. The author can be reached at pratikmba1@gmail.com

Other title by the Author

Learning Business Strategy through Case Study

The book is available in both eBook and paperback format on Amazon.in as well Amazon.com

https://www.amazon.in/Learning-Business-Strategy-through-Study/dp/1648925227/ref=sr_1_1?crid=3I94DJY4R6CZH&dchild=1&keywords=dr.+pratik+c+patel&qid=1604459673&sprefix=dr.+pratik+c%2Caps%2C342&sr=8-1

Caselets in Strategic Management

The book comprises of nine case studies on various topics of Strategic management.

1. Maruti Suzuki NEXA: An Exclusive Dealership to Attract Premium Buyers in India through differentiation
2. Hero Honda Joint Venture: A Great Friendship And A Graceful Separation
3. The Rise and Fall of Indian Iconic Car; "The Ambassador": A Case of Marketing Myopia
4. Kinetic Honda Joint venture: A Rare Failure For Honda: Lessons in Globalization
5. The Failure of Maruti Suzuki Kizashi in India: A Case of Strategic Blunder
6. Bajaj Chetak: The vehicle that held Indian families together for decades
7. The Tata Fiat Joint Venture: Fiat's Desperate Attempt to Revive And Establish Fiat Brand In India
8. Mahindra and Renault Joint Venture: Renault' Market entry strategy for Indian market
9. Tata Nano: A Missed opportunity for the world's cheapest car

www.ingramcontent.com/pod-product-compliance
Lightning Source LLC
Chambersburg PA
CBHW060852220526
45466CB00003B/1337